WHY WOULD ANYONE E

MW01104027

John Patrick Pazdziora, EDITOR
Katherine Langrish, FOLKLORE CONSULTANT
Defne Çizakça, FICTION EDITOR
Joshua Richards, POETRY EDITOR
ISBN 978-1-907881-59-6

Cover illustration by Laura Rae
Layout and typesetting by Eric Pazdziora
Typeset 12 by 14 in Adobe Caslon Pro

Unsettling Wonder is an imprint of Papaveria Press

www.unsettlingwonder.com

WHY WOULD ANYONE ENCHANT THAT?

Unsettling Wonder 2:1
Fall 2014

Fenioux : St Andrews

TABLE OF CONTENTS

Introduction..1
    by the Editors

Magical Object the First: Rubik's Confused............................ 6
    Thomas Brauer

Where Is That Magic?..7
    Jane Yolen

Lemon-Aid...8
    Sierra July

Annealing.. 17
    Sharon Dodge

Magical Object in the Middle: Fibonacci's Velodrome............. 27
    Thomas Brauer

Folktale: The Enchanted Teakettle.................................... 30
    Presented by Katherine Langrish

Hestia's Chair... 37
    Maureen Bowden

The Lady of the Loom... 47
    Benjamin Darnell

Dusting...56
    Sarah Ann Winn

Magical Object the Last: Plant Life.................................... 57
    Thomas Brauer

ELCOME BACK TO UNSETTLING WONDER. We've got a new volume and a new issue chock full with enchanted lemonade, magical teapots, and sinister arm chairs, as we ask ourselves the question—wait, why would *anyone* enchant that?

But, pan-dimensional Rubik's cubes notwithstanding, our theme today is not absurdism but realism. Lower that eyebrow—barmy wizards and daft witches enchanting the oddest work-a-day things is a matter of both serious realism and consequence. The enchantment of odd or banal objects touches the heart of the enterprise of writing: the rule of the improbable fiction.

Suppose that one of my students were to come to me, like the lawyer in Matthew 22, and say, "What is the greatest commandment in writing?" I would answer that "Aristotle says, 'What is convincing though impossible should always be preferred to what is possible and unconvincing' (*Poetics* 1460a, trans: W. H. Fyfe). This is the first and greatest commandment, and the second is like it: 'In character-drawing just as much as in the arrangement of the incidents one should always seek what is inevitable or probable, so as to make it inevitable or probable that such and such a person should say or do such and such; and inevitable or probable that one thing should follow another' (*Poetics* 1454a, ibid.). On these two hang the craft and the canon."

The impossible (*e.g.* wizards existing) is easily swallowed by readers. What isn't so easily swallowed is the improbable, *e.g.* wizards behaving in ways different than how they might imagine humans would behave with such powers. The infusion of the fantastic does nothing to abnegate—indeed, it rather intensifies—the responsibility to create real human beings. There are the old, high myths: Faust, Merlin, the Sibyl of Cumae, but our characters will as often say with Dante the Pilgrim: "I am not Aeneas nor Paul" as we, "I am not Homer nor Virgil."

No, the mass of humanity, and by extension the mass of fictional wizards and witches, are thoroughly pedestrian, preoccupied, for the most part, with ordinary worries, like turning on the automatic faucet in the public bathroom, or getting the rice to be ready at precisely the same time as the curry, or getting home in time to watch a rerun of *Law and Order* before Mom calls to see if we're eating our veg, or handing in the essay before midnight on the twentieth—not out of any harrowing desire to save one's soul from Mephistopheles but simply to save ourselves from ordinary embarrassment.

Which, if you think about it, goes a long way to answering why anyone would enchant anything. If you *could* have an army of flying monkeys to make the rice for you or set the DVR to record *Cheers* when you've forgotten or better still reassure Mom you're eating your vegtables—well, why *wouldn't* you? And if you can't afford even a modestly-sized regiment of flying monkeys due to the insurance, why not just pepper the apartment with lots of little cantrips—vegetables that eat themselves,[1] cooking pots that consult with each other and regulate their cooking time accordingly, automatic faucets that actually *do* something when you want them to?

As a wise man once said, the average person now carries more power and technology in their cell phone than was used on most of the Apollo moon missions—and uses it mostly to consult football results and find cute kitten pictures. So the enchantment of objects outside of the solemn tradition (keys, wands, staffs *et al.*) is humanizing in its way. To have magic at the fingertips and, without explicit, good reason, forbear is an improbable fiction. No less an author as Shakespeare had his greatest wizard, Prospero, use his powers mostly to test the mettle of his daughter's boyfriend (in a manner of speaking). Not even Faust himself bothered with conquering space and time with every burst of magic power: much if not most of his magical endeavours were to convince a nice girl to go steady with him, mostly, it seems, because he wasn't terribly adept at casual chatting and asking for phone numbers. Even in Tolkien, Gandalf uses magic for pipe-smoking and entertaining kids with fireworks. And what frost magician isn't going to use their powers to keep the beer cold on a summer day?

---

[1] The Poetry Editor apologizes if the General Editor's image of self-consuming and screaming-all-the-while cauliflower haunts your dreams. It does his...

In this issue, we have a startling array of strange enchantments for your delight and unsettlement. Jane Yolen begins the issue with a poem in search of workaday magic. Sierra July explains what happens when you get carried away when magicking pink lemonade, and Sharon Dodge guides us through the dark trails and enchantments of a story about loss, and aging, and love. Then Katherine Langrish introduces us to a very curious tea kettle—or raccoon—or something. Maureen Bowden discovered the haunted interstices between storytelling and interior design, while Benjamin Darnell weaves a tale of a clever thief and trickster. The issue concludes with Sarah Ann Winn's poem about a strangely haunted household chore. And running throughout the whole issue is Thomas Brauer's three part photo-essay on uncanny magical things.

Perhaps the issue may or may not answer the question of *why* anyone would enchant *that*. But certainly it will leave you eager to wonder: *what* should we enchant *next*?

John Patrick Pazdziora
Joshua Richards
Feast of the Transfiguration, 2014

This summer the roses are blue;
the wood is of glass.

MAGICAL OBJECT THE FIRST:
"Rubik's Confused
by Thomas Brauer

WHERE IS THAT MAGIC?

Jane Yolen

RITE ME A STORY where the magic flows
Through thimbles, toilet seats, thumbscrews.
Where the dark lord's soul is in pink handcuffs,
The hero's his eleventh toe.

I need a tale where the whole world hangs
On black metal pulls of a dresser.
A witch's powder puff spreads pandemic,
A wizard's shaved beard a forest.

Enough of wands, keys, cupboards, spells,
Familiar stuff we all have read.
We need tough magic fooling eye and ear,
Becoming extraordinary

Again.

LEMON-AID

Sierra July

 HE SKY IS PINK BECAUSE one little girl's lemonade decided to defy gravity and go up. Attempting to raise money to see her ailing mother to a hospital, Lem (named after Lemons, truth be told) concocted her own unique mixture. Selling plain old lemon juice and water just wouldn't cut it, not with the funds she needed.

Her mother loved lemons, healing fruit she called them, power to ward off the Devil in skin that smelt like sunshine. Plus, lemons fit in the hand like they'd fit in the heart, she'd add. Lem believed it, all of it. Because of her love of lemons, Lem's mother collected a menagerie of ingredients to jazz up her choice drink—lemonade. Ingredients based on those found in classic, and magical, literature.

"You don't dabble in what you don't know," her mother would whisper, her coal black eyes flashing. Even with no one else in the room, in the whole house, her mother whispered. It got Lem to thinking that the walls had ears tucked in them, or maybe the ghosts within the walls had more than air pass through them, had the ability to collect secrets and wrap them in their white pillowcase bodies. "You got to keep your wits, but you can't let your wits whip the fun right outta you." Lem would nod then her mother would bring out a Present. Presents were the special stuff.

Alice in Wonderland candy was Lem's favorite, the shrinking kind. Pop a candy heart in your mouth and you were mouse-sized. One afternoon, Lem explored the entire house that way, her mother watching to make sure the family cat didn't grab a hold of her. Lem worked on climbing a table leg, went for a swim in the kitchen sink, and sky-dived back down. Now the jumbo-sizing ones were junk to be wary of: a nibble and you threatened the roof above your head. Lem couldn't find much pleasure in feeling squeezed out and not being able to go out the door. The neighbors knew nothing of the Presents, the magic in them, and her mother wanted to keep things that way. So Lem should have known better than to scroll through the ingredients without permission.

The shelves were in the basement, shelves with vials pressing in on each other. Some were clearly labeled, while some had their brands rubbed off so that her mother must have known them the closest, known them by color and smell, perhaps even taste. Lem saw one she knew well—Hazel and Gretel witch gingerbread—and she avoided it like the plague. She didn't want to chub up any. Her mother made her eat that during winter, saying, "You're going to freeze in them usual skin and bones you carry. Meat and fat make you healthy and keeps your heat in." Good thing it was summer. Lem liked being in her usual skin and bones.

Lem explored a bit longer then settled on a vial. She took the one most pretty, one with golden dust that reminded her of her last year teacher's art time glitter, glowing specks to be used sparingly. Well, Lem thought, she could use however much glitter she wanted, especially her own, and the gold dust went into her lemonade, right after the raspberry juice and lemon juice and sugar. That gave her pink lemonade. Tiptoeing so as not to wake her mother, Lem set up for sales—table, pitcher, and cups—and didn't realize her mistake till she poured a glass, thankfully for herself and not yet a customer.

Her glass shook and the ice clinked as the lemonade spurted into the sky in a stream more powerful than a blasting water hose, magnetizing the juice in the pitcher with it. She had to squint up at it as the lemon acid made her eyes sting. Still, she could taste the wonderful tartness on her tongue with each breath. The lemonade tower scrolled further than she could see and spread across the blue and white before vanishing, staining everything pink, a masterwork both dazzling and terrifying.

What to do when the sky gets thirsty? That wasn't the real issue, only that she'd used Pixie Dust. Her mother had always said, "No you can't have that happy magic till you're good and old. Makes you so high you float, and can't come back down." It looked pretty up there, all that pink infecting blue nothing and cloud. The normally white cotton balls were now fleshy pink dislodged tongues. Lem considered overruling her mother, taking a swig of the forbidden juice and trying to capture the color somehow. Bread sucked up stuff. Maybe if she cooked up a giant loaf, sailed up there, stayed till the sogginess made her plop back down... No telling how long that'd take. That wouldn't be using her wits.

Lem went back to the basement and the shelves of vials. Was there one that would make a great whale of clouds that had a thirsting for juice? It could suck the juice up and shoot it high, high up with its blowhole, so high it left the sky, reached outer space and stayed there. If only it were that easy.

Again the dilemma of choosing a vial, some blessings, others more trouble than they were worth. "All necessary though," her mother would say, "all with their own purpose, own place, and own time."

So which vial's time was it to shine?

Picking blind was as good as gawking for hours, so Lem shut her eyes and made a grab. When she opened them again what she held in her hands was a vial with a rubbed-off label. It had dust caked on it, so Lem couldn't write off the worn label being from the vial's excessive use. Fact was it may have been a hand-me-down. Lem's mother got those from her mother, and her mother's mother. Inside was a murky brown liquid like swamp water.

"Here's hoping," Lem whispered, and popped open the vial.

Black swirls belched from the mouth and wrapped themselves around her. She suffered a coughing spell as a result of an egg-gone-rot stench, held her breath to quit it. When the smoke cleared, she was still wondering what the bottled swill did, far as she saw...nothing.

Then she felt something tickle her back.

She jumped, gasped as she saw that a white rat had fallen from her. It had landed on its rump and was looking around like a lost child. Another rested near her feet. At that moment a claw scrapped her ear. She shivered and swatted at her hair. A third rat plopped beside the others and the three got up and commenced bumping walls, sightless as newborns. Cuter on the ground, she let them go. The cat would at least have an easy meal tonight. Still, she knew this wasn't going to work.

Lem had no more answers and decided to bother her mother in bed. She hated doing that, waking someone weary who could hardly keep their head. She crept upstairs, tapping lightly on the door before walking into the shadows. The blinds were shut so her mother only had stripes of sun on her face. Lem had to smile because her mother looked like a zebra.

"Wakey, ma," she said softly. Her mother's eyes opened to her regular morning wake call. It was routine even if the time was off, normalcy despite the absurdity carrying on outside. "You feel good?"

"Feeling alright." Her mother blinked, too slow for a person that wasn't ailing. Lem didn't even know what her mother had, just that it took hold of her quick and didn't want to let go. "What you been up to today?"

"Nothing. Just… What if… if someone did wrong, but not too much of a harmful wrong, just wrong in the way it ain't natural?"

"Shit, I don't know what you're talking about, girl," her mother groaned. Her eyes were closed again like she was sleeping or dead, but sick air swamping her chest, coming out all itchy in her breathing, told Lem she wasn't either of those. Just pretending to rest and knowing she'd never be able to. "Speak clear, or get gone."

Lem swallowed. No use holding back now. Her mother had a sixth sense about these sorts of things. You start a conversation all sketchy one second and then speak too clear the next and you were lying, lying low as a dog, that's what she said. "I…I got some magic…stuck in the sky."

Her mother's eyes shot open, her lips churned like she was chewing fire. "You did what?" She spoke in that low voice, worse than any yelling.

"I was trying to help and things went wrong." Lem blurted. "Trying to make sales to collect money, money to get you hospital help, so you don't end up like daddy."

Lem expected her tongue lashing then, spittle flying and talk of disappointment and betterment tagging for the ride. Lem studied her feet, bare and much too small to be holding her up so full of sorry.

"You did wrong, girlie. But…but what do I say about your wits?"

Surprised, Lem recited, "Use 'em but don't let 'em keep me from fun."

"Right." Her mother smiled. "Sounds like you had yourself some fun. And I'm glad of that. How about you tell me everything now?"

Lem told her mother: the lemonade stand, the added Pixie Dust, the levitating drink and the rosy sky. Her mother laughed, astonishing Lem more. Today was beyond bizarre. Made her wonder if she was still snoring in bed.

"Well if you didn't about make it seem the sun was falling child." Her mother shook her head. "The sun... now the sun'd be someone else's business. The sky I can fix."

Her mother shuffled to swing her legs over the edge of the bed, getting ready to stand. Lem stumbled over to assist. Leaning on Lem, her mother got out back, down the stairs by some miracle and out into their sunflower garden. "What we going to do here?" Lem asked.

Yellow flowers dazzled Lem's eyes, all of them with their brown faces pointed at the sun. Lem's mother got down on hands and knees like she was searching for something. None of that made sense—coming out here, eyeing flowers. Lem was about to ask again what brought them to the garden when her mother said, "Ah now, here it is." She had got something clutched in her tired hands, something peeking out a peculiar color.

"What is that?" Lem asked. As her mother opened her hand, she saw. It was a sunflower, a blue-maned one. Its core was black. "That a sunflower too?"

"Yes and no," her mother answered. The smile she wore now was a sad one, a misty one. Her eyes sang the same song, sad and misty. "This here's a rainflower, one of a kind."

"Never heard of that in no story." Lem wrinkled her nose.

"Never been in no stories," Lem's mother said. "They come from anyone with a scrap of spirit. This one grew on your daddy's ashes." Lem's mother turned and studied her for a minute, seeming to find whatever she sought in her Lem's unkempt hair and knobby knees. She shook her head, grinning. "Just as if he knew what idea you had swimming in your head. This here's what we need."

One by one, Lem's mother plucked the rainflower's petals till it had a naked face. Not how Lem had seen her collect sunflower seeds, waiting until the petals were crackly and the seeds in center were black and white. A small tear scrolled down her mother's cheek as she took the black heart of the rainflower and shred it to bits. It looked like dandelion fluff with its color inverted by the time she was done. Fluff to her lips, Lem's mother blew for all she was worth.

The fluff flew higher and higher till it disappeared. The sky was still pink lemonade dyed, no sign of changing.

"What good did that do?" Lem asked.

"Just watch." Her mother was staring at the sky. Lem did the same. Those lolling tongues of clouds were morphing, mashing themselves into one angry bunch, gone from blushing pink to red.

"What's happening to 'em?" Lem backed away slowly, ready to run but not knowing where to. Blood-red clouds looked like a nightmare.

Then she noticed something. Patches around the clouds were reviving, going blue again. The clouds were soaking all the pink from the space about them like leeches. They swelled and swelled till they were more like water balloons, a low rumble gurgling in their throats. Lem could smell the citrusy tang, again packing her nose so strong that she could savor the flavor. Soon as the clouds were so red they looked black and the sky was azure, they crumbled like balled-up paper, squeezing themselves, sending a thick sheet of rain plummeting. Lem opened her mouth to receive it. It tasted like lemonade from God's own kitchen.

"Well, that put all nature's laws in order," Lem's mother said, hands on her hips. Lem hadn't seen her look this strong in months. Lemonade slid off of her and gave her tired skin a soft glow, her soul light. She would still be needing hospital but, just for an instant, she was cured of feeling sick. She was happy. All thanks to her daddy's own magic. "No real harm was done." Lem was being ushered inside, drenched to the bone but never feeling so good. "Guess now all we got to worry about is explaining to the neighbors."

Lem's mother hobbled inside after her, giving Lem time to gaze out at the lemonade rain still falling, the sun making each drop gleam like a firefly's rear. In the sunflower garden, she thought she glimpsed something, a new glint of blue in a sea of yellow.

Lem dashed back outside before her mother could forbid. Her joy was bubbling so much she had to. Raising her arms, Lem lifted her head and twirled, whooping as lemon rain bathed her.

ANNEALING

by Sharon Dodge

HE DAY MY MISTRESS MADE ME, the ocean was too quiet. All was a soft, silent gray. A gentle, tired kind of color: even the air, lethargic. She should have waited for a great storm to make me, she said, should have waited for a whirling, vibrant tempest. That would have made me stronger, younger. Then I would have been able to save her, as I was meant to do. Instead I was useless, the magic buried deep—her own fault, she would admit, in less angry moments. Her fear keeping her from the bold attempts that might have worked.

Here is the story: there once was a beautiful princess with secret powers that lay humming under the skin. A witch from far away saw her, and loved her, and drank the power from her until she thought the well was dry. But some magic remained, and with it, the princess cursed her lover to an existence as cold as her witch's heart. She wished the witch's skin to grow cold and lifeless until her whole body should turn to glass. And so my mistress, the witch, created me to save herself.

When I was born her hands still held a shadow of warm, spongey flesh, her face a faint hint of human wrinkles, but they soon faded into the cold transparency of her glass-cursed body. She was more beautiful then, but it was a hard, granite kind of beauty. The magic still lay strong within her fading bones; but she was never able to pull the old sea-magic from within me, nor I give it to her.

I was not beautiful, of course—my eyes a wet and mutable blue, my skin as perfect as the beach's dark sands that she drew me from. I was devoid of human expression, of freckle and hair and pulsing blood beneath. I was ugly, perhaps, but I was not old. But I suppose she was right to call me so. Who is young that has never known youth?

Before the earth-child came, the witch and I sat in the garden by the pond. Sometimes we would talk of how we would break the curse, but most days she was too tired to even pretend; still recovering from my birth, she explained.

"And little good it's done me. Barely more than a scullery maid I've managed, and not even one I'd care to bed," she growled to the open air, as though I didn't sit with her. "Magic buried so deep she herself can't feel it." She tipped her wine glass back and drank lustily; she ate little lately, but drank no less. Her glass nails flashed in the sun with the gesture, scintillating lifelessly, and I wondered if I should apologize.

"I could go to the princess and beg for your forgiveness," I said, pulling an apple from the tree above us, marveling at its rubicund face. "I could bring her offerings and sit at her door a thousand days and nights until she is convinced of your repentance."

"Yes, very helpful," she said, "very useful of you to be far away from my aching bones. Besides, it doesn't matter; she will not forgive me. She cannot," she sighed. "No, it is we who must fix things, we who must find some healing thing," she said, her empty wine glass held tight to her chest.

"You are getting weaker," I said.

"I will find a way," my mistress responded.

For a while I believed her—what else had I known? We gathered the garden flowers, the vegetables which she picked at during mealtimes. We watched the lonely stars. She grew a little stronger again, began telling me about the heavens and their order, almost happy, despite the paleness of her face. We pretended I was her apprentice, that her curse was soon to be overcome; that sweet times were ours.

"I thought you would make me whole again," she said to me one day in our cramped parlor. "But we are better this way, mistress and apprentice. I will teach you the language of the sky, and you will tell me what your sea-blood whispers. But," she added, smiling, "for now, I'll simply show you how to build a fog-wraith."

She was surprised by her own interest in me. Her amusement with my clumsy ways, her cold delight with her own superiority. And yet I do not blame her. I suppose I was built to love her—although perhaps not the way she wanted, though I did not know this at the time.

I learned my first true lesson about mistress on the day I found her working the deep magic. She must have been preparing through the night; how she had mustered the strength to glide so quietly, I never knew. She was smiling, the faintness of her body beautiful that day, rather than painful.

"This is a tincture of the twenty-third element, that most useful and elegant metal. It comes from the stars and brings much power to a potion." She started talking as soon as I walked in, her hands flurrying out about her, her long robes swinging. "Quickheart root for intensity, and sun's ray for enduring affection, and clean feathers for quick action; add to the metal—" She choked her words, and her eyes gleamed for a spare second. She seemed almost human again then, but with a malicious undertone I had forgotten. Cackling as she finished, she drank the smallest sip of the potion, then raced past me to crush the pestle and its mixture into the fire, her fingers blistering glass bubbles. The vessel cracked and shattered, and the metal shone. We waited in silence as the flames flickered.

We waited, though I did not know for what; I stood, blank and uncomprehending, for my mistress's magic. Some minutes passed.

"I do not feel it," she whispered, her tongue languishing in her gently-parted mouth. "Why don't I feel it?" she asked, her voice straining.

"What, my mistress?" I asked, my eyes trained on the perfection of her mouth, aching to touch it, though I did not know why. She stared back at me, mouth closing—stepped back—and raised her arm.

I screamed when her hand hit me, for it was now harder than mortal flesh and heated, and her glass nails scratched deep into my skin, where it bled seawater. She stared at her hand, then cried out as it abandoned all humanity and grew smooth and transparent, as bereft of human character as the poorest of statues. Her eyes turned to me in panic. I left her to cry glass tears that would shatter on our warm hearth. In the morning I would sweep them up, and wonder at their expressiveness.

It was daily worse after that. Some days she was apologetic, even charming; but mostly, she was silent, morose, even sullen. And then one day, when the winter grew deep and the garden too cold for our picnics, she told me not to disturb her, not even to bring her food. It was then I realized she no longer needed to eat. My memory of that waiting time grows faint, like a view of the distant horizon greeting the ocean. Time passed, and I waited, alone.

Cobwebs grew upon me—I had no need for human movement—as I sat beside her door. When my mistress came out again, she handed me a robe the color of rich earth painted with leaves and branches and told me to go find the girl. She said nothing else. Her hands touched mine, cold and perfect, and I saw there was almost nothing human left under her hood—her last magic spent in building a second savior. I rose from the dust and the world went quiet. I went to find her new creation, searching in the forest west of us.

I suppose I have never really trusted the soil. I am a creature of water, of change; the earth is slow to move, rebellious and recalcitrant. The forest does not trust me when I enter, and so I went but rarely, and only with my mistress. The world around me was too quiet, the songbirds timid, the insects hushed. Only the wind kept on, and the hum that ran through my head and called me forward. The wind asked me silly questions: Ocean-mother, why now? and When does Summer come? We miss her games.

I would not answer her. Instead I searched the earth, bending to let my fingers enter and find the hum beneath its surface. In truth, I disliked being called mother, I who was so new.

The earth was soft and loose beneath my palms; the forest so young, the ground almost as rich and perfect as my mistress's garden. I wondered if the girl beneath it was afraid, and dug my fists in deeper. The hum intensified; perhaps it was now audible to the forest. For to me it thrummed, hammered, rang. The world around me lapsed into utter silence—and then, my arms buried to the shoulder, I touched her wooden hand, and shuddered.

It was not supposed to happen; maybe I was simply lucky. Or perhaps we never truly understood the nature of the curse— I only know the new hum of my skin, the brightness of the sky, and how I am thankful, and sad.

She came up out of the ground laughing, the whorls of her chestnut skin warm against my hand and then my chest as she all but fell on me, her cherry mouth red and inviting. As she began to speak, so did the earth. To my relief the repressive silence vanished as the birds began to sing, the insects returning to their respective songs and dances. She curled a hand around my face, eyes too wide.

I took her hand and gently pulled her after me, a leaf in a river, a mischievous dragonfly in the mistress's garden. She would not let go of me, but her hands wandered; always a finger touching this and that, here stretching out to her utmost, there pausing to catch a bit of sunlight peaking through the forest roof. My mistress had picked a young green place for her birth: too young, too bright. My magic was too deep, unreachable, but this girl's was unripe; my mistress would never survive the drinking of it.

I tried to mourn my mistress's death in that moment, but I was not so human yet, and it was all too far away. I wondered if my mistress would see what I did in this tiny creature. I was already less young then, in light of the earth-child's dance; I felt my age settle about my shoulders. I considered hiding her, telling my mistress the spell had failed; but perhaps she'd find her anyways, and the scars on my face were pearlescent still. I thought for a moment, just a moment, that I would like to see my mistress's final collapse. At the thought, I checked to see if my hands had turned to glass.

MY MISTRESS HELD THE GIRL. She petted her, she spun her around the room with glee; but she did not see her as I did. I sat in the corner of the room, drinking saltwater out of a silver cup. The girl delighted in the wood of the house, the garden, the colors of the sunset; and I said nothing, but watched and waited as the sun went down.

The next morning I was waiting beside her when she woke: she was frightened, rolling off the bed, eyes wide—and then she laughed, sat up, fear as absent as the night. She was older already; growing much faster than I. But then, I was never so young. She drank, tasted; a little fruit, a few nuts, but never more than a few bites. She watched the world out the window with wide eyes, though not quite so wide as yesterday, until she finally spoke.

"She is sick, isn't she?"

"As a sunflower in the dark," I said. "She was a witch-woman, and was cursed by a princess who loved her. Now she grows as cold as her heart once was. Even her unexpected kindness to you cannot save it. She is not, was not, a good woman."

"But you stay with her."

"I do. She made me such."

"Why did she make us?"

I looked at her bright eyes. "I'll tell you tomorrow," I said. But as it happened, I didn't.

My mistress did not leave us much time together—from then on there were duties. She made as if there were some grand spell to prepare, and I did not tell the earth-child of the falsity of this. The last charm was cast; my mistress was only waiting for its fruition, for the honeyed tongue of the earthchild, for the cherry mouth that bound it. My mistress was burning the last bit of her candle with a desperate fire, and she was beautiful.

But the earthchild did not notice. I suppose we were all blind, a little, for until she woke me in the night with her sweet mouth and dark eyes, I saw her no better than my mistress did. Only then in her soft-grain arms with her mossy hair about us did I fully let myself see her.

Our magic must have filled the air, more potent than the blossoming roses, for the morning had barely broken when I found my mistress hovering over us, though my beloved still slept. She came and sat on the bed, stared at our entwined limbs and the softness of our now-human skin, smelled the rich female scent that thickened the air. I tried to muster some dislike of her, and found only a blankness.

"I should have gone to find her, but I was too weak," she murmured.

I touched the new texture of my skin. "The magic is spent. I can no longer help you; I am sorry."

"But you would have it no other way," she said.

"No," I murmured. "It was you that would have it this way," my throat stung suddenly, and my eyes. "Was I so strange and old?" I asked. "That you could not love me, even with love potions and loneliness both?"

"I should have waited for a storm," she said.

"And now," I said, "there is no magic left in you, save curse. And you will die."

She nodded, but did not look at me.

I felt something break inside, and I wished to speak over its horrible crashing, but could not find words. She left us there, her movements strained and harsh.

It was some weeks before we realized that she had not only ceased to speak to us, but to speak at all. After that, she grew slower still, some mornings spent without a single movement, watching the now-dead garden out of her unblinking eyes. The cold no longer troubled her. One day she forgot to dress, her clear figure as absent of detail as the rudest of statues, sitting idly in the winter's sun. We built a bench for her, and covered it in soft pillows; she sat and drowsed, seldom moving. One night we came to sit with her, the snow cradling her in its own blanket; by the morning she breathed no longer.

My anger cooled with her transition, to the point that I am mostly sorry when I look at her. We are thinking of going to the east, to sail beyond reach of sight until we find some little island, where we will both be happy; although sometimes, we speak of visiting the princess. The house is almost closed up; we are taking very little. Although my beloved says not to, sometimes I cry, though less for my mistress than for myself. I wish, I always wish that our beginning had been less un-kind—but the wind is singing, and my beloved's mouth tastes of honey, and I know that sorrow is not long.

MAGICAL OBJECT THE SECOND:
Fibonacci's Velodrome
by Thomas Brauer

27

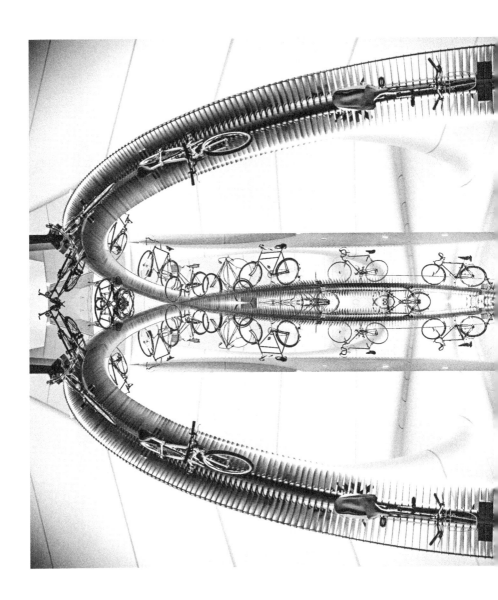

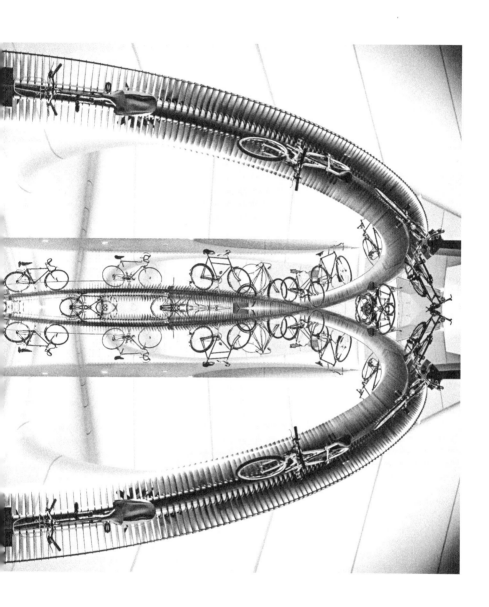

29

WELL, WHY *WOULD* ANYONE ENCHANT THAT?

Katherine Langrish

HY? WISH-FULFILMENT IS ONE ANSWER. Fairy tales are practical things, made up and told by practical people. A magical crown, sword or ring is all very well, but not half as useful as an enchanted version of the sorts of objects used by people every day.

If it takes cold, weary hours to trudge to the nearest town, what more natural than to wish for boots which could take you leagues in a single stride? And if all you have for protection is a cudgel, what a comfort if that cudgel were a magic one, which could beat your enemies into submission while you stood safely at a distance!

When life is hard, when food is scarce, what better than a little table

> which was not particularly beautiful, and was made of common wood, but which had one good property; if anyone set it out and said: "Little table, spread yourself," the good little

table was at once covered with a clean little cloth, and a plate was there, and a knife and fork beside it, and dishes with boiled meats and roasted meats ... and a great glass of red wine which shone to make the heart glad. [1]

And then it clears itself afterwards so you don't even have to wash the dishes.

Wish-fulfilment is not to be scorned. Someone, at some time, said, "How cold it is! I wish we could tame fire! If only we could have a little one burning all the time, to cook our food and keep us warm!" Someone else said, "Grinding grain is weary work. Do you see how strongly the wind blows and the river rushes? What if we could harness their power to turn our millstones?" Much more recently, someone said, "What if we could make a horseless carriage?" And we're still at it. Driver-less cars... self-cleaning glass... solar panels sitting on the roof... The what-ifs of this world, prompted mainly by discomfort and the desire for an easier life, have been the mainspring of human invention. And invention is the stuff of fairytales.

But there's more to it than wish-fulfilment. These stories aren't naïve. They're intended to amuse, and much of their success is due to the conscious manipulation of incongruities. A powerful djinn is shut up not in a golden casket, but in a common, earthenware lamp. The Gold-Ass in the story of the Wishing Table spews golden coins out of its mouth—and its backside.

Further, the tales remind us of the magic of everyday life. All gadgets are magical gadgets; until we become too accustomed to see the magic right there in front of our eyes.

31

Finally, the stories warn, treat your magical gadgets with respect. Used moderately and with wisdom, they will help you get on in life. But use them carelessly or greedily, and disaster will follow. Remember what happened to the Sorcerer's Apprentice: don't kill the goose which lays the golden eggs. So read the instructions, remember the magic words. Or the enchanted salt-mill may just go on grinding and grinding until the entire sea is salty...

In the Japanese tale that follows, *The Magic Kettle* as retold by Mrs Lang, a poor man finds a kettle which is inhabited by a spirit-animal, a tanuki or raccoon-dog. In fact, the tanuki *is* the kettle, the kettle *is* the tanuki. The story's sense of fun and wonder is well expressed by the Japanese title, *Bunbuku Chagama*, which apparently translates as "happiness bubbling over like a teapot". I hope you enjoy it. And—remember: that electric kettle sitting on your kitchen counter? It really is enchanted, you know.

You've just forgotten that you couldn't boil the water all by yourself.

---

1 Grimm, *The Wishing-Table, the Gold-Ass, and the Cudgel in the Sack* (KHM 36)

THE MAGIC KETTLE
From a Japanese folktale, adapted by Mrs Lang

IGHT IN THE MIDDLE OF JAPAN, high up among the mountains, an old man lived in his little house. He was very proud of it, and never tired of admiring the whiteness of his straw mats, and the pretty papered walls, which in warm weather always slid back, so that the smell of the trees and flowers might come in.

One day he was standing looking at the mountain opposite, when he heard a kind of rumbling noise in the room behind him. He turned round, and in the corner he beheld a rusty old iron kettle, which could not have seen the light of day for many years. How the kettle got there the old man did not know, but he took it up and looked it over carefully, and when he found that it was quite whole he cleaned the dust off it and carried it into his kitchen.

"That was a piece of luck," he said, smiling to himself; "a good kettle costs money, and it is as well to have a second one at hand in case of need; mine is getting worn out, and the water is already beginning to come through its bottom."

Then he took the other kettle off the fire, filled the new one with water, and put it in its place.

No sooner was the water in the kettle getting warm than a strange thing happened, and the man, who was standing by, thought he must be dreaming. First the handle of the kettle gradually changed its shape and became a head, and the spout grew into a tail, while out of the body sprang four paws, and in a few minutes the man found himself watching, not a kettle, but a tanuki! The creature jumped off the fire, and bounded about the room like a kitten, running up the walls and over the ceiling, till the old man was in an agony lest his pretty room should be spoilt. He cried to a neighbour for help, and between them they managed to catch the tanuki, and shut him up safely in a wooden chest. Then, quite exhausted, they sat down on the mats, and consulted together what they should do with this troublesome beast. At length they decided to sell him, and bade a child who was passing send them a certain tradesman called Jimmu.

When Jimmu arrived, the old man told him that he had something which he wished to get rid of, and lifted the lid of the wooden chest, where he had shut up the tanuki. But, to his surprise, no tanuki was there, nothing but the kettle he had found in the corner. It was certainly very odd, but the man remembered what had taken place on the fire, and did not want to keep the kettle any more, so after a little bargaining about the price, Jimmu went away carrying the kettle with him.

Now Jimmu had not gone very far before he felt that the kettle was getting heavier and heavier, and by the time he reached home he was so tired that he was thankful to put it down in the corner of his room, and then forgot all about it. In the middle of the night, however, he was awakened by a loud noise in the corner where the kettle stood, and raised himself up in bed to see what it was. But nothing was there except the kettle, which seemed quiet enough. He thought that he must have been dreaming, and fell asleep again, only to be roused a second time by the same disturbance. He jumped up and went to the corner, and by the light of the lamp that he always kept burning he saw that the kettle had become a tanuki, which was running round after his tail. After he grew weary of that, he ran on the balcony, where he turned several somersaults, from pure gladness of heart. The tradesman was much troubled as to what to do with the animal, and it was only towards morning that he managed to get any sleep; but when he opened his eyes again there was no tanuki, only the old kettle he had left there the night before.

As soon as he had tidied his house, Jimmu set off to tell his story to a friend next door. The man listened quietly, and did not appear so surprised as Jimmu expected, for he recollected having heard, in his youth, something about a wonder-working kettle. "Go and travel with it, and show it off," said he, "and you will become a rich man; but be careful first to ask the tanuki's leave, and also to perform some magic ceremonies to prevent him from running away at the sight of the people."

Jimmu thanked his friend for his counsel, which he followed exactly. The tanuki's consent was obtained, a booth was built, and a notice was hung up outside it inviting the people to come and witness the most wonderful transformation that ever was seen.

They came in crowds, and the kettle was passed from hand to hand, and they were allowed to examine it all over, and even to look inside. Then Jimmu took it back, and setting it on the platform, commanded it to become a tanuki. In an instant the handle began to change into a head, and the spout into a tail, while the four paws appeared at the sides. "Dance," said Jimmu, and the tanuki did his steps, and moved first on one side and then on the other, till the people could not stand still any longer, and began to dance too. Gracefully he led the fan dance, and glided without a pause into the shadow dance and the umbrella dance, and it seemed as if he might go on dancing for ever. And so very likely he would, if Jimmu had not declared he had danced enough, and that the booth must now be closed.

Day after day the booth was so full it was hardly possible to enter it, and what the neighbour foretold had come to pass, and Jimmu was a rich man. Yet he did not feel happy. He was an honest man, and he thought that he owed some of his wealth to the man from whom he had bought the kettle. So, one morning, he put a hundred gold pieces into it, and hanging the kettle once more on his arm, he returned to the seller of it. "I have no right to keep it any longer," he added when he had ended his tale, "so I have brought it back to you, and inside you will find a hundred gold pieces as the price of its hire."

—*The Crimson Fairy Book*, Edited by Andrew Lang
New York: Longmans, Green, and Co., 1903

HESTIA'S CHAIR

Maureen Bowden

Y BOYFRIEND MARK AND I WERE bargain hunting
in our local flea market when we found the armchair.
"Look at that, Anna," he said. "It's perfect for your
flat."

The pink and purple floral upholstery was stained and
faded; stuffing, that could have been horsehair or something
nastier, poked through the backrest; a spring had popped out
of the sagging seat like a jack-in-the box without a head. "It's
disgusting," I said.

"It's shabby-chic."

"No, it's shabby-sick."

"You could put a throw over it."

"More likely throw up over it. It looks as if someone
already has."

We didn't notice the stallholder until she placed her bony
hand on my shoulder, and whispered in my ear, "It's cheap."

Startled, I stifled an expletive, and turned, to look into large, deep-set eyes, sunken cheeks, and a wide mouth, full of teeth. She brushed back strands of grey hair that had escaped from the knot on the top of her head. "How cheap?" I said.

"How much have you got?" I delved into my pocket, and produced three pound coins, a fifty-pence piece, and about a quid's worth of shrapnel: just enough to stretch to a couple of cappuccinos in Starbucks. The skeletal fingers moved faster than Batman's fist on the Joker's jaw, and left me gazing at my empty palm. "You don't want it wrapped, do you?" she said.

Mark and I dumped the monstrosity in the back of the clapped-out Ford Transit van borrowed from his dad. "Right," I said. "You're buying the coffee."

That evening, we manoeuvred the chair into the alcove next to the electric fire. "I think we were robbed," I said. We headed out on the town for a Saturday night drink or six. Mark was paying. We picked up a takeaway pizza for supper on the way back to my flat and then I packed him off home. We both knew I'd let him move in with me sometime soon, but for now I was enjoying my solitude.

The following morning I slithered out of bed at eleven a.m. The ghost of Kurt Cobain was grinding out Grunge in my skull, my mouth tasted like a vulture's crotch, and an un-welcome caller on my doorstep had a finger wedged on the bell. I opened the door and the stallholder who'd sold us the chair said, "Cultivating the wind-swept look, Anna? Put a comb through your curls, girl. You've got a visitor. May I come in?" She looked different. Her long hair flowed loose around her shoulders. It wasn't grey, but silver, in the morning sunlight. She was old but beautiful, the way crackling logs, glowing embers, and a sunset at the dimming of the day are beautiful. She was also transparent and hovering about three inches above the ground.

Without waiting for a reply she drifted into my combined living room and kitchen. I followed, wondering what the hell kind of orange juice was in all those Brass Monkeys I put away last night, and why it hadn't worn off yet.

She glanced at the unwashed dishes in the sink, the overflowing litter tray growing its own eco-system, and my evil cat, Camilla, snoring on the table between a half-eaten pizza and my laptop with something sticky drying on the keyboard. "Nice," she said.

I ignored the sarcasm. "OK, I know you're not real." I fished the paracetamol out of their home in the breadbin, rinsed the least objectionable cup under the cold-water tap, and swallowed three. "But just to go with the flow, what are you?"

"Writers call me the Muse. I've also been called Antropus, Peg Powler, Ginnie Greenteeth, the Cailleach, Black Agnes and Morgan le Faye. I quite enjoyed my incarnation as the Fairy Queen: out of character, I know, but Bottom was a hummer in the hay." She winked. "I've been mistaken for the Virgin Mary once or twice. She and I had a good laugh about that. Most people, however, don't call me anything, because they can't see me."

Lucky them, I thought. "What do you want me to call you?

"Hestia. Goddess of the Hearth."

"So, you're not human, then?"

"Not likely. I wouldn't be one of you lot for all the weed in Eton."

I scooped up three tee-shirts, two pairs of jeans, and assorted underwear, from the couch, slung the lot on the floor, sat down and hugged a cushion. "I know you'll disappear when the pills kick in, so according to the chemist you've got six minutes to tell me what you want."

She turned her eyes to the armchair in the alcove. "I see you chose the right place for my chair: at the fireside."

"I'm not sure it's stopping. It's a heap of junk."

"No, my dear. It's the second most valuable thing in your life."

"Why?"

"Because I've placed a spell on it."

"Why would anyone want to enchant that?"

"To provide a link with the World of Story. You're a writer, I believe."

"I'm doing my best, whatever other people think. We all have to start somewhere."

"Well, you have to convince them. Long ago, folk would have called you a storyteller. All the best tales were told in my domain: at the hearth. The Power of Story lies with the denizens of fiction. They are elusive, but they can be found. My chair is a link. Use it well."

"Why have you given it to me?"

"Not given: loaned. I've loaned it, for a small returnable deposit, to many writers."

"Anyone I'd know?"

"You'd know Will Shakespeare, I presume, Hans Christian Andersen, Jane Austen? Dear Jane and I became great friends." She floated to the kitchen table and examined my laptop. "Jo has one of these," she said.

"Jo who?"

"Rowling. Hers is cleaner."

Camilla woke up and hissed at her. Hestia gave her a look that would freeze a fish finger faster than Captain Birdseye could pile on the ice. The indignant beast leaped out of the open window, no doubt intent on showing next door's tomcat a good time.

"I'll clean it," I said.

"Good. I'll leave you now, but I'll return soon to observe your progress."

"Before you go, tell me, if the chair's the second most valuable thing in my life, what's the most valuable?" She smiled, and vanished.

I approached the link to the denizens of fiction, and sat down, avoiding the headless jack-in-the-box. The chair seemed to fold around me, soft, warm, and protective.

I closed my eyes and every tale I'd ever been told, every novel I'd ever read, every play and every film I'd ever seen, poured into my consciousness. Fairytale characters spun gold, stole porridge and made their way to Grandma's house stalked by the Big Bad Wolf. Huckleberry Finn; the March sisters; the inhabitants of Middle Earth, the Discworld and Hogwarts; Beowolf; Captain Corelli; and everyone in-between, played out their lives for me. I saw the characters in the story I was trying to write. I laughed with them, danced with them and soaked up their lives. But from the corners of my eyes I could see shadows. I turned to face them and they transformed into fingers of fog that clouded my vision. I sensed viciousness, terror, despair.

I flung myself out of the chair, and knelt, retching, on the floor. I pulled myself to my feet, ran to the bathroom, and vomited in the toilet bowl. No more Brass Monkeys for me, I swore. I lay huddled on the bathroom floor until the nausea subsided, then I showered, dressed, drank three cups of coffee and forced myself to eat a round of buttered toast.

With the images from the World of Story still chasing each other around my brain, I sat on the couch with my sticky laptop, and started to type. The characters that had been hovering at the edge of my consciousness for months became words on the page. I wrote all day and I knew I was writing a story that wanted to be told.

Next day, filled with the conviction that I was entering a new phase of my life, I was cleaning Camilla's litter tray. I sensed Hestia's presence before she spoke. "You've seen the shadows?"

"Yes. What are they?"

"What all humans have within them: the aspects of their nature that they seek to deny. You have to learn to control the shadows."

"I'd rather keep away from them."

"Then you can't be a writer. If a dark story needs to be told you must tell it, but there are dangers."

"What kind of dangers?"

"They can mess with your mind. The Brothers Grimm plunged into the darkness and almost lost their way. Wilhelm coped but poor Jacob took a hammering. He became a recluse, you know. And Edgar Allan Poe went off his trolley." She laughed, with rather too much relish, I thought. "Although he was always a few spokes short of a wheel, of course."

"They made me sick," I said.

"Even Shakespeare threw a wobbler in his early days. Are you familiar with 'Titus Andronicus'?"

I nodded, fighting back another bout of nausea. "If he couldn't cope there's no hope for me."

"He did cope, and that's what you have to do."

"How? Give me some hint!"

"An innocent soul is the best protection. The shadows will bow to it, acknowledging a power greater than theirs." She took my hands in hers. "Go where your stories take you, Anna, and don't be afraid." She vanished, and she still hadn't told me what was the most valuable thing in my life.

I'm a down-to earth sort of a girl and these events were freaking me out. I needed to talk to someone, so I asked Mark to come over. I told him about Hestia, about the World of Story, and about the shadows making me sick.

He didn't interrupt, but when I'd finished he shook his head. "It isn't real, Anna," he said. "It's all in your mind, and it's my fault. I shouldn't have persuaded you to buy that damn chair. I'm so sorry."

I knew it was real but I understood how it must have sounded, so I didn't argue. "Perhaps you're right," I said, "but whether it's all in my mind or not, it helped me to start my story and I've got a good feeling about that. One other thing: when can you move in?"

He grinned, "Now-ish?"

"One condition: I've been living like a slob. We need to give the place a good clean. You up for it?"

We spent two weeks making the flat fit for human habitation, and turfing out my hoard of rubbish, including, a full set of *Buffy the Vampire Slayer* magazines; four sole-less pairs of fake Ugg boots bought on eBay (I never learn), and an unassembled self-assembly bedroom set, minus the screws. We crammed it all into the rotting shed at the bottom of the yard. "The local kids can take it for their bonfire next Guy Fawkes' night," he said.

"They might as well take the shed, too."

We settled into blissful co-habitation: a storyteller, a potential astrophysicist studying for a Ph.D., and a cat with attitude. Life was good and it was about to get better.

I was writing. The story was unfolding the way is should and I knew it was good. The day I completed it I called to Mark, "I've done it. The story's finished." He twirled me round in his arms and lost his balance. We tumbled on to the couch, nearly flattening Camilla, who'd staked her claim to it after we'd banished her from the freshly scrubbed kitchen table. She yowled a feline curse, but refused to budge.

"What the hell was that?" he said,

"We sat on the cat."

"About the story: what happens now?"

"I suppose I try to get it published, but I can't wait to start on the sequel."

"You don't need the chair, Anna. You won't use it again, will you?"

"Just one more time."

"I wish you wouldn't."

"I'll be fine. I promise."

I wasn't altogether sure of that, but I wanted to do it before I lost my nerve. It would be difficult with Mark around, worrying about me, so I waited until he went to a lecture at uni. I sat in Hestia's chair, holding my laptop, and I closed my eyes.

The shadows saturated me with darkness. I breathed it in. It filled my lungs. I saw an image of it entering my bloodstream and travelling to my brain. It showed me what it held: princes shrunk and wrinkled into frogs, children abandoned in the forest, and evil queens tearing out their rivals' hearts. It showed me Lavinia, raped and mutilated, blood dripping from the remnant of her severed tongue and the stumps from which her hands had been hacked. It showed me Madeline, screaming, entombed alive in the vault below the house of Usher. It showed me Sophie, forced to choose which of her two children would die in the gas chamber. The images faded but the shadows still surrounded me. They bowed their heads and then they retreated. I opened my eyes and started to type.

Next morning I awoke with a headache so bad that I couldn't get out of bed. "Have a lie-in," Mark said. "I'll bring you breakfast in an hour or so."

I drifted in and out of sleep, before waking to the smell of burning. A trickle of smoke sneaked through the open window from the yard, and I knew what was happening. I threw my bathrobe around my shoulders and ran outside in my bare feet. Mark was feeding the rubbish from the shed onto a bonfire. Hestia's chair was blazing on top of it.

I screamed, "No, no, you can't. It isn't mine."

He pulled me into his arms. "I had to, Anna. It was making you ill."

I was sobbing against his shoulder when I heard Hestia's voice. "Don't worry. Fire can't destroy it." I turned, to face her.

"You're real," Mark said. He was trembling, but his voice was angry, rather than afraid.

"How can he see you?" I said.

"He thinks you're as far off your trolley as Edgar Allan. We have to put him straight."

"What do you want?" Mark said. "Why can't you leave her alone?"

She ignored him. "I've come for my chair. You don't need it anymore." She pointed at what remained of the second most valuable thing in my life, and it vanished. "You faced the shadows and they bowed to your will."

"Yes, but why? I don't think I qualify as an innocent soul."

"You don't, my dear, but your daughter does."

I stared at her. "What?"

Mark said, "She's pregnant, isn't she?"

"Of course, she is," Hestia said, "and I'll be expecting an invitation to the birth. I'll be there anyway. I turn nasty if I'm not invited."

"You're invited," I said.

She nodded. "Take care of her, Anna. She's the most valuable thing in your life. Oh, in case you're interested, the cat's pregnant too. I hope that motherhood will improve her disposition." She grinned, and was gone.

Mark hugged me. We held each other close as the fire burned itself out. Three pound coins, a fifty-pence piece, and a quid's worth of shrapnel were lying in the ashes: just enough to stretch to a couple of cappuccinos in Starbucks.

THE LADY OF THE LOOM
Benjamin Darnell

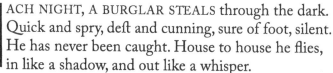ACH NIGHT, A BURGLAR STEALS through the dark. Quick and spry, deft and cunning, sure of foot, silent. He has never been caught. House to house he flies, in like a shadow, and out like a whisper.

What does he take, you may ask. Does he line his pockets with jewels? No. Does he take the silver? The gold? They could surely be bartered with for a handsome return at any of the town's vendors. No. Is he a grumpkin, on the hunt for naughty children to snatch and gobble up? Hardly. Or is he just a poor beggar, cold and hungry, in search of food and warmth? Still no.

He serves a mistress, The Lady of the Loom, and her tastes are quite specific. She asks only that he bring her a single thread from each person living in each house he visits. She is spinning a tapestry, you see. A beautiful, magnificent tapestry that the eye would quiver to behold. And in due time, the burglar will receive his just reward, she assures him. A treasure greater than any he could spend in an entire lifetime.

The Lady of the Loom sends out her thief. And she weaves.

We do not know how this arrangement began, but since its inception, the burglar has crept through every house he could reach before the rise of the sun, even the Queen's castle. Now, one might think the castle so tight and so well-guarded that not even the most skillful thief could breach its walls, and certainly, the Queen was of a similar mind. And why should she not be? For nothing of any great value to her ever turned up missing. But such is the stealth of our burglar that he skirted the guards each night, extracting a measure of thread from each of their uniforms. He then floated to the Queen's very chambers, where he snipped just what length The Lady required from the spools tucked away in her handmaidens' quarters, Who would be any the wiser to such a robbery? Who would notice such a thief, such a phantom in the night?

It just so happened that on one particular summer evening, when the burglar delivered the thread to his mistress, always weaving, weaving, weaving, he ventured to ask, "My Lady, all these years have I been your loyal servant. All these years have I done just as you asked, each night refreshing the stock of your loom. When, might I ask, will my services be complete? When will I receive my just reward, as you promised?" Whereby, The Lady looked up from her loom and, composed, said, "My loyal servant you have been, but I cannot give you your reward. It is something that you must find for yourself."

That, as you can probably imagine, was not at all what the burglar had wanted to hear. Enraged, he stamped and shouted at The Lady, "I've been deceived! You never intended to give me any payment at all, did you? You're nothing more than a vile woods-witch! I'll not waste my time with the likes of you again!" He stormed from the clearing where The Lady sat at her loom, and all the while she wove. And all the while, she smiled.

The burglar was disgusted. All the time he had spent collecting thread for her when he could easily have become rich off his skill; it irked him. He fumed, but then it came to him. He knew exactly how he would compensate for all the time he had wasted.

And so, the next night, he did not sneak into any houses. He did not steal any thread. That night, he had his eyes set on the Queen's castle, and only the Queen's castle. He would slip in, and he would not leave until he had taken enough to make him a wealthy man. The first part of his plan went off without a hitch. He evaded detection from the guards easily, just like any other night. And just for the record, if you are thinking that these guards ought to be sacked straight away for their sheer incompetence, I assure you they really were quite vigilant, and quite well-suited to their post. No other burglars had ever broken in, had they? It's just that our burglar is so gifted, and so practiced in his craft, that avoiding detection had become mere child's play for him at this point. Loading up a sack full of gold, jewels, and heavy trinkets, and keeping quiet, however, had not.

The metals did clang and clatter against one another in the sack. To say that it made a terrible racket would be an exaggeration, but it did make more than enough noise to alert the guards, who came at once and descended upon our burglar in the Queen's drawing room. There, you see? Not at all incompetent.

Needless to say, they confiscated their captured thief's stolen goods and locked him in a dungeon cell until the Queen awoke the following morning. They brought him before her in the throne room, where he promptly dropped to his knees and groveled at her feet. "Please, Your Majesty... p–p–please have mercy. I—I'll never steal again, I promise."

The Queen, who had not had a prisoner to sentence for quite some time—her guards were rather effective at keeping the peace, I'm sure you'll understand—decided that she would have some fun with this one. "Rise," she said. "I will offer you my pardon, but first, you must do me a service. No one has ever broken into my palace before. Therefore, you must be an exceptionally skilled thief. And I currently find myself in need of a thief of exceptional skill." Our burglar was listening intently. "As you have seen for yourself, I have all the wealth I could ever want. I have gold. I have jewels. I am rich beyond measure. I will never go cold or hungry, and I have an army of servants at my beck-and-call every minute of the day. But there is one thing I desire that all of my money has not been able to buy—time.

"You see, I am not as young as I once was. My youth is escaping me. People tell me—because they are smart—that they cannot see it, but I know it is a lie. I see it. I feel it every day when I rise from my bed—in my back, my feet, my neck. I succumb to the affliction of age. You, thief, steal me back the time that has escaped me. Restore to me my youth, and I will restore to you your freedom. You have until tomorrow, and if you do not return, my guards will hunt you down, and you will spend the rest of your days rotting in my dungeon."

Our poor burglar did not know what to do. Who could steal time, after all? No one, that's who. Time was not something you could hold—something you could pluck off a shelf, stick in your pocket, and be off into the night with. It was obvious that the queen expected him to fail. She just wanted to watch him squirm with an impossible task before locking him in the dungeon forever. Perhaps he could escape—run off somewhere far away where the Queen's guards would never find him. He was, after all, quite adept at evading them when unencumbered. It was a possibility. But before he resigned himself to a life on the run, there was one person he thought he ought to ask for help.

He beseeched The Lady of the Loom, still seated in the forest clearing, still weaving. He begged her forgiveness, and told her what had happened at the castle. The Lady listened, silent, weaving. He asked if she would help him complete the queen's task. "She wants me to steal back her time that has been spent," he explained. "But how can such a thing be done?" And then, desperate, "is there any magic that you could—"

"My loom runs low," she cut in. "You brought me no thread last night, and soon I will be unable to weave the tapestry."

"I—I'm sorry, I... what if—" our burglar was grasping for a solution. "What if I bring you twice the thread tonight, to account for the night I missed? Then, will you help me?"

"See that it's done."

It was done. The burglar had never been so swift, so quick, so nimble. He stole twice what The Lady normally asked of him from every house. He even snuck back into the castle—a prospect that was wholly unnerving, as I'm sure you can imagine—and came away with twice the armful of thread, silent as the night.

He gathered all the fabric in a bundle and laid it on the ground before The Lady, just as the sun was rising and just as she emptied her loom. "Here you are," he said. "Twice the usual. Now, will you help me?" The Lady smiled and ran her delicate hands over the tapestry, extracting threads as she went. Once she had unraveled a fair handful, she offered them to our burglar. "Here," she said. "Give the Queen this."

The burglar stared at the threads in his hand. They were of fine quality—the finest quality, actually—so they could only have belonged to the Queen. But this would not do. "This is not what she asked for! How will this help?" He was outraged.

"You have asked for my help, and I have given it," said The Lady, suddenly stern and terrible. "If you do not want it, give the threads back." Our burglar was cowed. He made his way back to the castle, clutching his offering and wishing he felt more hopeful.

The Queen was not pleased. She shouted that this was not at all what she had requested, as our burglar knew she would. She called the threads an insult and said that now, not only would he be imprisoned, but also flogged every morning, because on top of everything else, he had just revealed that he's stolen even more from the Queen than she knew. She snatched the ball of thread from his hand, and was just ordering that he be thrown into the dungeon's darkest cell, when she froze.

She was staring intently at the bundle as though it were the most extraordinary thing she'd ever seen. Her guards asked her what was the matter. She said, "I feel... younger!" She called for a mirror to be brought immediately, and when it arrived, she delighted at her reflection. "My skin, it's smoother! It glows more than before! There are less spots, I'm sure of it! You!" she turned to our burglar. "Thief, where did you get this—no, nevermind that. Is there anymore? Can you get me more?" She was shaking his shoulders. A wild look danced in her eyes.

Our burglar assured her that he could get as much as she wanted, and she told him that so long as he did, he could keep his freedom. He went back to The Lady of the Loom that night, after making his rounds, as usual, and she unraveled more of the Queen's thread for him to bring her the next day. The Queen was ecstatic, and she asked him to bring her more the next day, and the next, and the next one after that. On and on.

Each day, as the Queen accepted the next bundle of thread, she was a little bit younger. She said that her back no longer ached, that her feet no longer hurt, and that her neck was no longer stiff. Before long, she looked as though twenty years had fallen off her. But not all the change was good.

With each passing day and passing gift of the magic thread, it was becoming increasingly obvious to the Queen that something was wrong. Every day she looked younger, but she also was beginning to feel less and less. There was an emptiness growing inside her which she could not explain. She felt somehow diluted, like wine mixed with too much water. Until one day, she gasped in horror when she held up her hand and found that she could see right through it.

The next morning, when our burglar came to deliver the thread, she had her guards seize him. She confronted him with such ferocity that he shrank in fear from her youthful face. She insisted that the threads he gave her were cursed, that he had tricked her and was plotting to have her killed. She demanded that he take her to wherever the threads were kept and reverse the spell, lest she call for the executioner to take his head.

The burglar did as he was told. He led the Queen deep into the forest, where The Lady of the Loom sat in her clearing, weaving as always. Weaving, weaving weaving. "You," the Queen said in a voice quivering with rage. "Look what your witchcraft has done to me!" She showed The Lady her hand, which was still transparent, like a ghost's. "I command you to lift this curse at once!"

"That, I can do," The Lady said serenely. "But you must first give me that dress you wear," for the Queen had ordered her servants to fashion her a beautiful dress from all the thread that had restored her youth. She cast it off now without modesty, and thrust it at The Lady. And The Lady unraveled it, and little by little, wove the threads back into the tapestry.

As she worked, the queen's body became solid again. The emptiness inside her was filled. But her youth was fading all over. Her skin began to sag. She felt wrinkles form around her eyes. All the aches and pains returned. "No," she whimpered. "No, not again. I can't bear it! Stop!" She ripped the needle and thread from The Lady's hands, and the threads that had been woven back into the tapestry, she tore free once more, until all the threads that had comprised her dress were now in her hands. But she did not stop there. In her frenzy, she tore out all of her own threads that she could find, even those that had not been removed once already.

And she, the Queen, sank to the ground, weeping, with her bundle of thread. Until, as she held it, her youth was magically restored once more, and her sobs transformed into laughter. It is hard to say whether or not she noticed that as her age was again fading, so too was her body's form—I imagine she must have known it would happen—but she continued to laugh as she became less and less, and even less, until finally the only thing left of her was her laughter being carried swiftly away on the wind.

The Lady smiled gently, took up her needle and some new thread, and set about repairing the tapestry. "It is a terrible thing, to waste time dwelling on the past," she said to our burglar. "Those who do can never truly live in the present." And he looked at the tapestry, in all its magnificence, and he saw that it was beautiful. And on that night, and every night until his last night, he gamboled off like a shadow, and he brought her thread, and The Lady wove, wove, wove.

DUSTING

Sarah Ann Winn

Scooping up the dust and chanting "Live!"

S SOFT COLORLESSNESS is glossed away,
the memory in things returns, rises
when she swipes her cloth, or lifts a little

wood-carved hound from his place on the mantel.
Passing across the mirror's face restores
a face which once appeared over her shoulder,

startled her dusting. The words spoken
undustable; and yet, the spell, persistence
in tending, suffices—reanimates the love.

MAGICAL OBJECT THE LAST:
Plant Life
by Thomas Brauer

A feather is all it takes
to make me die laughing.

Lightning Source UK Ltd.
Milton Keynes UK
UKOW07f0959310515

252613UK00008B/33/P